Calculated Hesitation
Mary Grace van der Kroef

Copyright © 2024 by Mary Grace van der Kroef

All rights reserved.

Cover Art:
"Contemplation" ©2024 Mary Grace van der Kroef, Ember van der Kroef
Watercolour Painting
All Rights Reserved

Edited by: Kirsten Pamela McNeill (Worthy Writers Editing)

ISBN:
978-1-7777211-9-0 (ebook)
978-1-0691537-0-8 (paperback)

First Edition

Contents

Titles By Mary   VII

1. Hesitation   1

   Hesitation

   Above Self

   Be Quiet

   Unknown

   Coming About

   Gift of Time

   Breath's Imprint

   Drips of Me

   Starving Over Time

   I Know He Cries

   I looked

   Present

   Night

   Off

   Open Fear

    Pinched Sight
    Rarely Found
    Winds of Words

2. Art   29

    An Artist's Weapon
    Art
    Artistic Intimacy
    Catch a Muse
    Colour Tells Stories
    Gleaning
    Grow A Rhyme
    Uncracked Spine
    Residue of Muse
    Beauty of Forgetting
    Shards of Heaven
    In Between
    Thought's Vine
    When I Write A Poem

3. Defiance   47

    Hey Trouble
    Comply with the Lie
    Ink Pens
    Simple Security

    Cotton Candy Lies
    Whispered Fists
    Dying Dreams
    Emptiness: A Beginning
    Sound of Silence
    Tantalizing Thing
    Paper Telescope
    Words That Stick
    That Night
    Lights On
    Matured Whims
    Reaching for the Sun
    Used Cup

4. Resolution   79

    The Weight of Me
    Home Over Walls
    Spoken Secret
    Lace Curtain
    Unhindered
    Peace Seeds
    Did We Ask
    Hold Hope
    Look Beyond

Wake Up

Words of Life

Calculated Hesitation

Acknowledgements   98

About the Author   99

Poetry:

The Branch That I Am

Words of Weight

Branches in Bloom

Fiction:

Our Road to Trust:
Interlocking Short Stories of Faith

How We Love Them:
A Hope is Here Novel
(forthcoming)

Visit www.marygracewriting.ca for more information.

Hesitation

This heart has slowed
longs to linger here
where the past is distant
the future unclear

A hesitancy
to pick up life's pace
a straining to remain
firmly in place

Give me grace

Unlike a crossroad
where choices must be made
more like a settling
a sinking in of ways

Smell the resignation
come wafting on the wind
stagnation that lingers
on boots and trouser hem

Mix it with the drums
foreboding rhythms felt
clashing with a heartbeat wearied
yet compelled

Standing mid the street
holding baggage fast
wondering how long
this lump in throat will last

Change
coming
fast

Above Self

Like a heavy hand upon my back
Reality smote its prey
And self flew away
Whisked about by solar winds
Above a body numbed by pins
Silence
Was the weight spirit clung to
So as not to drift
Holding back
From eternities rift
For an inkling of time, there was a freeing of mind
Blackness
Soft and fine
Then a yank
Back in line
Unaware of the sublime
In between
A blink
Grasping at thoughts that walked away, feeling a hole
Losing what had been
Grieving ghosts
Forgotten sin
Slipping back to what's always been
Again
In self

Be Quiet

I ask them to be quiet
Thoughts within my mind
I ask them to be quiet
For they are not kind

I ask them to be quiet
It's time to take a rest
I ask them to be quiet
My peace is now oppressed

I ask them to be quiet
But it is to no avail
The nonsense they are shouting
Has risen high in scale

I ask them to be quiet
My voice in whispered rounds
Under their swelled insistence
My plea is nearly drowned

I ask them to be quiet
For I fear I will forget
There is peace within my heart
Despite their daily threat

I ask them to be quiet
So many times a day

I ask them to be quiet
While I tell you, I'm okay

I ask them to be quiet
Though I'm tired of the strain
I ask them to be quiet
Pray that they'll soon wane

I ask them to be quiet
Even as I understand
They are my own cries
Once muffled, now at hand

Perhaps it's time to listen
Despite this painful muse
Perhaps the lies are really truth
Throwing out its cues

So I'll ask them to speak softer
Sort them one by one
I'll try to find their meaning
Ask for peace when I am done

Unknown

It's terrifying
Falling into the unknown
But it pulls eyelids down
So much could happen
With the loss of consciousness
I battle rest
It always wins
Forge into sleep
But wake up weak
It's terrifying
Facing the illusions of day
Work or play
The ache is never gone
Need collects
At an eye's edge
A crusted pledge by a body
Return
To the unknown
Even while hands grope
For solidity
In this waking world of lights
Shadows
Mirrors
Faces that rarely show honest emotions
It's terrifying
Living

Coming About

It's a difficult thing
coming about
shifting positions
turning around

Humbling questions
confusion galore
but brave souls
can also restore

An off kilter compass
foot steps astray
brave hearts can hold
pride at bay

Utter "I'm sorry,"
cry when they pray
know, failure
is more than okay

Gift of Time

A sigh for self
a tired plea
a longing
to be set free

In-drawn breath
exhale slow
with it, release
internal foe

To sit and breathe
receive time's gift
to meditate
emotions sift

Send them out
acknowledged whole
taking in peace
that chaos stole

Breath's Imprint

Give pause for breath
Another for death
Wait for ringing bells
Listen for crashing swells
While in-between
Lean forward

Anticipate change
While greeting the mundane
Support
Spur on
Knowing none have long
Yet impact is strong

Even if only one soul remembers
The sparkle
Behind eyes
It lives forever
As lessons pass on
To generations

Futures
Of shared breaths
That rise to winds
Ringing bells
Rippling the surface
Of life

Drips of Me

Data swimming
in a pool of liquid

She, a drip
a fluid orb spilled across a cheek

Momentum gained
over skin slick with oil

Suspended struggle
before release of toil

A mixing
gain and loss, living race

Smallest drip
hold worlds

Against a face
falling through space

Starving Over Time

I miss friendship's caress
The playfulness of nudge
Without it my heart is lonely
My days an aching trudge

I miss compassion's touch
Cupped in empathy
Knowledge only passed
In arms of sympathy

I communicate my love
With handshake, hug, and kiss
When it's been withheld
I feel I am dismissed

Even though right now
To gather is a crime
I fear for every heart
Starving over time

I Know He Cries

As I looked into his eyes
I saw he often cries
You may not see his tears
But he's been spilling them for years
They don't run down his face
They leave no tracks, or trace
Unless you're looking deep
You'd never know he weeps

I spied them in his glance
It was caught by chance
A blink and it is gone
I saw it beneath his brawn
That glimpse was all it took
Knowing where to look
Every time we passed
Those tears cut me like glass

Spilled and forever chilled
Ice daggers thrown when willed
He threw one out at me
That first time made me flee
I confess to giving ground
Walking another way around
I didn't want to face
His disdain with my disgrace

As time passed along
I felt this choice was wrong
Took another turn
Walked his way unspurned
I met him that bright day
He almost stepped away
But in offering my hand
I showed I meant to stand

His grasp was firm but brief
A second's deep relief
As our handshake broke
I watched his eyes uncloak
I wished him a good day
Turned to go my way
But then his whisper heard
Turning back, my heart was stirred

I watched a dagger melt
Saw the pain its falling dealt
As down his cheek it slid
That single tear soon hid
But pain he did not fear
Now his gaze was clear
He thanked me for my grace
Appreciated a smiling face

As we parted ways
Thankful for his icy gaze
It was not as it had seemed

Beneath I saw
With truth it gleamed

I looked

I looked
but didn't see
blossoms bloom for me

Too long to study hands
dream
of untried plans

I looked
but was too late
time the petals ate

As I looked
seconds rolled
forever they are bold

I looked
now what I see
fruit upon the tree

Gifts as seasons pass
but
is it mine to grasp?

Hesitation
yet again
watched a harvest plain

But looking
isn't reaching out
time forgives no poet's doubt

Present

How difficult to be present
Live in the moment unrepentant

Struggle to not look back or ahead
Hold a single experience instead

How difficult to turn off noise
Of a mind overwhelmed by toys

Really hear the words you say
Have the desire to join your play

Difficult, but impossible? Not
Not when freedom is truly taught

A conscious choice to carve out space
From modern glitz and words that race

A present self, a soul in place
Let my mind be touched by grace

Night

Night is not my time of fear
Sometimes it helps the air to clear

When all is quiet and needs rest
My heart and head work at their best

When day is like a blaring noise
I often seem to lose my poise

Night, it brings a softer song
A respite from the milling throng

In the quiet I can hear
My heart recite what it holds dear

Held together by His word
Recalling truths, my heart is stirred

Then my mind it gives the nod
And in agreement we are awed

Forever in the hand of God
Through these days, onward I plod

Off

Where did I go
a moment ago

My mind drifted
upward it lifted

When it came back
I felt the lack

A hole in thought
an empty black spot

Am I still me?
Change, could it be?

Or did I grow
before I could know?

Strange to be
yet not to see

Somewhere there
but unaware

Should I care?
say a prayer?

Send a flare?
or forget the affair?

Open Fear

Ears that bleed
Eyes that stream
The waking world
A nightmare dream

Where is truth?
Hidden away
We the people
Are fear's mass prey

It stalks the world
Both day and night
The silent streets
Stroke appetite

The howl heard
By young and old
We don our masks
Resignation unfolds

The seance of danger
Is strong and thick
Fanned by media
paid by clicks

Fear now gloats
Walks the day

Knows no shame
At our dismay

Behind four walls
We find a peace
The rich forget
Hunger won't cease

Our precious ones
We lock away
Keep them safe
Urgently pray

But danger finds
A way within
Steals them, flashing
Fear's wicked grin

How can we win
This unfair fight?
Fear has no favourites
All know its bite

I may not see
What path to take
It chills my blood
So much at stake

But one thing
I will not fear
I'll never cease
To hold you near

Pinched Sight

I saw fear
the slither of snakes behind irises of slate blue

Glimpsed pain
smiling
it's wicked teeth barracuda sharp

Noticed desperation
as it sat
a quiet shadow

Pinched
at the corner of sight
and knew it wasn't right

I shook hands
with resignation
sweaty palms gave it away

I could have
slapped
poison lies
made them ooze
from harrowed eyes

But
I let them walk away

I lost you on that day
I'm sorry
my own fear won its way

Rarely Found

I have always sought connection
That few know how to give
Yet, it is ever vital
So how can they all live?

I have always sought friendships
Deep, and steeped in truth
Rarely have I found them
I left them with my youth

Or was it an illusion
The bonds that once held strong?
Only for our younger years
Then they were all gone

I've often searched for links
Within a stranger's eyes
But what I have found there?
Well intentioned lies

I must ask the question
Could the absence lie with me?
Have I forgotten something?
Have I misplaced the key?

Do I offer up a friendship true
Free of all its traps?

Or have I also offered only
Meager time and scraps?

I'm unsure of the answer
My acquaintances would give
It's time for stepping back
Reassess and then forgive

I'm still looking for that friendship
Despite loves that I hold dear
I pray that I will find it
As I learn release of fear

Winds of Words

Can you hear words on the wind?
Whispers
"See you after work."
"I love you."
Through hushed tones
Echoes of things breathed out
Sucked in
"Not today, please ..."
"I hate you."
A mix of what makes us proud
"I made it!"
And what shames us most
"You're fake."
Would we say those things
If we knew they floated on the wind?
The bluster blows
And no one knows
Just how far our words will go

An Artist's Weapon

When my soul is too tired
To pick up a brush
I know it's for words
I must wait, with no rush

When the words come
Garbled and frayed
I know it's the brush
That should be my blade

An artist has weapons
They wield when dismayed
That holds back the darkness
Make it afraid

They are Heaven's warriors
Wielding a pen
Ushering in boldness
With brushes, they blend

Offer understanding
While battling life's storms
Remind us of beauty
In the middle of its norms

In the quiet, their message
Can bring sweet relief

Or sound the alarm
While using a motif

To be part of their guild
In my own small way
Is like Heaven whispering
I have your back in this fray

Art

It's the rhythm
It's the rhyme
It's the flow within a line
It's the music
It's the muse
It's the meanings you will use
It's the vision
It's the dream
It's the purpose driving theme
It's all within your heart
It's YOU, doing your part
It's giving back
It's art

Artistic Intimacy

Fingers that never touch
Yet
They dance in mirrored flight
As eyes take in the beauty
Of a love
Shared each passing night
With every page that's turned
Every line that's traced
Every note that's strummed
Strings held
In tight embrace

How intimate the artistry
Birthed
From a human heart
Entwining all that partake
In things we name
As Art
Sharing in connection
Linking spirits and minds
Becoming us
As we share threads
Heaven weaves and binds

Catch a Muse

Comes the breeze of experience
Comes a muse in its wake
Reaching up with open arms
Opportunity now to take
Snatch it from life's flow
Hold on to wriggling tails
Don't let go, no matter how
This muse fights and flails
Winds of change prevail
Grip could soon rip wide
Take heart, don't fall apart
This muse may help you glide

Colour Tells Stories

Colours tell stories
Of glory
Of worries
Of caresses
Of cold
When they are muted
When they are bold

Colours tell stories
In reds
In blues
In yellows
In greens
In rainbows of hues

Colours tell stories
Without use of words
No phrases
No questions
No verbs
To be heard

Colours in places
Words fear to tread
Needing no human
To help them all spread

Look for the colours
In dots
In specks
In flutters
That whisper of
Shimmers of red

In brightness
In shadows
Or under a rock
Yes colour
Unexpected
Will secrets unlock

Gleaning

Tonight I gather
picking bounty from others' words

Gleaning
as I watch, wait, and learn

Plucking experience
to stow
safe in pockets

Like berries on a bush
tinny succulent fruits

Some are bitter, some are sweet
all with bursting flavours greet

Many is the harvest if
one will reap
the moment's gift

Grow A Rhyme

If only I could finish you
Simple words, but still too few
If only words also grew
Like planted seeds covered with dew

Then maybe I would have a chance
To see this pen and paper dance
See my thoughts and words advance
Plant, then grow and show my stance

Maybe it has yet to climb
Did I forget to grow takes time?
So plant the seed, await the rhyme
It could reach bloom at anytime

Uncracked Spine

You
Meet me
In pages of cream
Through ink dark as dreams

Books beg to be read
As their pages whisper
Syllables of loneliness

Love me
As I love the touch of your hands
On my uncracked spine
Choose me

Let me linger in your mind
As slow sipped wine

Once the pages open
Words walk through soul
Hook, to your whole
Tethering stories
To what makes
You

Residue of Muse

sometimes
I slap the muse away
not liking how it looks
but when I do
it sticks to my fingers
a punishment
unrelenting residue of thought
so I'm caught in that thought
until it's realized
or drys up
leaving me parched for its fulfillment
wondering
what could it have been
chastised by lingering doubt
shamed by unwillingness
to see past
first appearances
you would think
a poet knew better

Beauty of Forgetting

First the sun bleached its vibrancy
To subtle whispers
A mural of marked moments disappearing
Through existing

Redraw the lines
Splash colours fresh
Upon the wall
For red to leak
Where pink alone has walked

Blue holding yellow's hand as
Fresh green parades between
Look
It's not quite as it was before
A shift

Mourn this change that steals
Celebrate what it reveals
In vibrant presence
A portrait restored
As memories

What is forgotten fades
What is remembered enhanced

Shards of Heaven

in a moment
with a motion
snapping fingers
holding time
hear a psalm
slip away
into a world
of the sublime

ask no questions
of the quiet
in between
the rhythm snap
let its pull
feed the wonder
giving answers
metre map

comes an ending
to the journey
settle back
into the skin
taking with you
shards of heaven
memories
a dreamers win

In Between

Love of spaces in between
hidden beauty
elements unseen

Holding life with silken thread
together
in a spider's web

Where all connects as if by plan
overlooked
by daily man

Yet spied if standing still
threads glisten
in sunlit thrill

Reaching through shadows deep
dipped in ink
strands creep

Gossamer, spun through air
touches all
love, wear, share

Thrumming tones reverberate
just beyond
each ear's gate

Only heard in whispers hush
heaven's voice
doesn't rush

All the spaces in between
breathing life
into this dream

Thought's Vine

Plant a word
to grow a thought
possibility
becoming plot

Plot twines round and round
until the vine is anchored down

Contemplation's roots have spread
deep inside mind's earth
and fed

Fed upon a life that's lived
diverting nourishment that's sieved

Between tinny stretching strands
moments
memories
discerning plans

From a single word
inspiration commands

When I Write A Poem

When I write a poem
I set out on a journey
With each step
I find myself more concerned with truth
Than with being clever
I pay more attention to sound
Than to sign posts
Catch myself doubling back
To smell the roadside daisy
Forgetting if I chose
The northern or southern track
I often find the starting point
Just to begin again
Reliving emotions
That drag new trails of thought
Across my path
Following them again and again
Testing if it leads me down the same roads
Or if by re-evaluation
I can find the hidden door to Heaven

Hey Trouble

Hey Trouble
I caught your glare
Though now you wear
That vacant stare

Hey Trouble
I know you blame
Everyone
But your own name

Hey Trouble
I see you hide
Behind the mask
Of selfish pride

Hey Trouble
I saw that flare
I caught that tear
Despite the glare

Go make trouble
When you're done
When the games
Have lost their fun

Come back Trouble
Now we'll make

A lesson from
These paths you take

Turn trouble
Back on its heels
Change that name
That binds, conceals

Goodbye trouble
Don't come back
This one knows
I have their back

We all know trouble
We all partake
But we're both done
With being fake

I saw trouble
Walk out the door
Now life can start
I name you, More

Comply with the Lie

eyes whisper
don't even try
while lips smile a wicked lie

comply

unspoken rules
used as tools
dividing dreamer from the dream

hidden regime

waiting for the trip
willing one to slip
to retain power's grip

on what's allowed

knowing well
how games are played
by silver words betrayed

arrayed

in tolerance
and glitz romance
mesmerizing trace

hide the lie

encourage comply
because all rely
on power

to suppress or to survive

Ink Pens

bravery in pen work
truth of staining spots
tells the story of a heart
stocked by fear
but still uncaught
every stroke
a slash at past
seeks to sever
cords
that grasp
the only sword that has a choice
to further peace
through language voiced
still leaving stains
on those who wield
the heavy tool in open field
not blood
but ink is what it weeps
into fingerprints
it seeps
brave
to name this sword a friend
knowing well it will offend
and mark the poet at its end

Simple Security

simple security
is never quite that simple
see

honestly honourable
some people find
intolerable

constant commotion
keeps the world
in motion

deepest devotion
wine?
or deadly potion

consuming confusion
birthing full
illusion

of misguided musing
while truth
we are abusing

twisted testimony
believed
by every crony

sides simmering
destroying
splintering

simple security
is never that simple
see

sadly slipping
beyond our hope
of gripping

worthy, willing
honestly
it's chilling

to see us filling
our hearts with pathless
milling

Cotton Candy Lies

Beautiful eyes
Beautiful lies
Pain as sweet
As sugar with dyes

Ingest the lies
Cotton candy replies
Ignoring aftertaste
For a moment of highs

Sick on lies
An empty prize
So beautiful but
Not at all wise

Whispered Fists

Whispered words
of ill intent
fly
like fists in hatred sent

Slither
into open ears
steal
away unopened tears

In their place, drop poison doubt
the seed of fear
is soon to sprout

Chokes
a heart in desperate need
to whispered fists, it will concede

Inside
a heart so wrapped in chains
hatred grows
quickly reigns

Soon the fists
don't need to hide
attack
defend
tighten pride

Mutterings
from the past
grow
to words that cut when cast

The carnage whispered fists have sown
damage done
a heart now stone

The first to whispered fists create
already lost
their war with hate

So consumed
they spread the grave
convinced their campaign
is well and brave

All fail to see the truth that hides
behind hatred's
staining tides

No longer on opposing sides
despite contempt
they are allies

Calamity's army
grows by one
understand this war
is far from done

How many more
will have to fall
before we hear Him softly call

Dying Dreams

Once bright
Full
Vivid
Now grey
Shrivelled
Decrepit
Once a bloom
Ready
To open
Now a dying
Lying
Thing
Crumbling
Despite the spring
Drifting
On shifting winds
Ashes
Pulled from my hands
Falling
On barren lands
Trampled beneath feet
Desiccated
Beyond belief
Empty
With open palms
Waiting

Dreams
Fertilize this path
As they die
Hope is cast
Unforeseen
Winds spreads the seed
Feet that trampled
Pressed seeds deep
Rain
From heaven fall
Nourish
As grief calls
Why?
When?
How?
When sunshine warms
Saturated earth
Sprouts burst

Emptiness: A Beginning

Emptiness
Whiting out
Blotting up the mess
But left alone
It is a throne
Of utter loneliness

Emptiness
A freeing find
But only for the brave
The clutter gone
Now be strong
Or line a bleached out grave

In Emptiness
It's possible
For newness to begin
Choose, create
Or open gates
Let possibility win

Sound of Silence

Hush
Can you hear it?
A softness in the night

Hush
Close your eyes
This sound is pure delight

Stop
Don't give up
Sit a moment and regress

Stop
Now breathe in
Silence is a caress

Find it
That feeling
Like waiting with intent

Find it
Uncomfortable
Yet sweetness in its get

Strange
To hunger
For what you easily break

Strange
To anticipate
Loss within its wake

Blessings
In finding
Peace in moments lent

Bounty
Bestowed
In silence well spent

Tantalizing Thing

Did you find it?
That thing you look for
That essence evaporated in the wind

It leaves a hint in its wake
To tantalize and tease
Hooking you into the chase
Becoming a need

Can you feel it?
A pull that never stops
As it forms a bone-deep ache

Reach for it
Catching hold of a tail
It slips away
As smooth as silk ribbon

Perhaps you're not meant to hold it
Until the campaign is won
Let it tug

Tantalizing thing
A reminder there will be more
Beyond our end

Paper Telescope

They handed me a paper
Said to show wonders
Distant truths
Spelled out

Recycled
Up-cycled
Between soft and rough
I follow instructions
Sculpting
Their makeshift truth tool

Peering through the tunnel
Focused on one point
Would it reveal distant revelations?

Restricting
Conflicting
Hyper focused in the end
What kind of message does that send?

Something's missing
There's a twisting deep within
As I realize
This telescope needs a lens

Words That Stick

Toxic waste
Blackened paste
Words that stick
Hearts defaced

By sludge abused
Forever bruised
Beneath the crusting
Phrases used

Unclean thing
How they cling
Defy attempts
To shield the sting

Leprosy
Our legacy
Every man's
Dark felony

Guard the tongue
From speaking dung
Words once said
Can't be unsung

That Night

You refused to come further
Than a foot inside the door
It was there we sat together
In our pile on the floor

I held you in my arms
Heads together, tears flowed
As we shut the door against
Early January's cold

We sat there for an hour
Then, another one, made two
All that time, I was praying
As I held on tight to you

This time was different
I was so afraid
I knew your many words
Meant things were really frayed

Your voice came out muted
Difficult to understand
So I just said "I love you"
Holding tightly to your hand

I felt something breaking
As you asked to use the phone

The answer brought only pain
I could hear it in your tone

So I kept my silence
Even though I wished to scream
Not knowing what to say
It all felt like a dream

After so much waiting
You felt it time to act
I watched with beating heart
As your pockets were unpacked

Sifting many layers
Finding secrets you kept close
Then pressed into my hands
Realities cold dose

The reminders that I held
Felt like an evil curse
I heard a cord inside me snap
Things would now get worse

I could only watch the horror
In your eyes resignation reigned
I saw your soul in torment
I knew it truly chained

As you walked away
I called into the night
"You do not go alone
God is with you in this fight!"

A single wave goodbye
As you wiped away a tear
Off into the night
I watched you disappear

A frantic turning point
A night so filled with pain
So much lost, so much cost
Never again can we reclaim

Alone even when together
Our worlds so far apart
But still we're friends forever
Even then with breaking hearts

We each now carry scars
That life has on us laid
Each know our own darkness
As with our tears we've paid

But every one we shed
I refuse to now regret
You are worth every one
None could I forget

Lights On

Waiting by the window
watching a silent phone
tonight I'll leave the light on
in hope that you come home

I wonder if you're hungry
I fear that you are cold
there may be snow tonight
for that's what I've been told

Putting on the kettle
I'll heat an extra share
it's the least that I can do
to show you that I care

The hour's growing late
but I wait a little more
maybe I'll hear you
come knocking at the door

The water has gone cold
my cup is empty too
I shed a tear
leave the light as hope for you

I'll leave it on tomorrow
again the coming day
each night I bow my head
in silence, I pray

The darkness may have hold
of someone that I love
but, God sent out his angels
they're watching from above

I asked Him to attend
help to keep you safe
until the day you feel
your addiction's chafe

When you're ready leave the needle
with the darkness that it holds
when you wake up in the night
to realize you're cold

I pray that you remember
there's someone at the gate
you don't have to fight alone
from beneath those heavy weights

There are battles to wage
and I'm ready to stand
beside the heart I love
the battlements are manned

I'll leave lights on forever
I'll never give up hope
I'm waiting for your call
I'll help you climb this slope

If only you come home

Matured Whims

Pour it out
Watch them swim
These thoughts
These frenzied whims

Squirm
As you watch them be
Stirred by
Reality

Tested under
Pensive gaze
Peeling back
Ignorance's haze

Experience
Solidified dreams
Witness growth
To realized schemes

Shadows
Or seraph wings
What evolves
Bind with strings

For whims grounded
Uncontrolled

Can multiply
A hundredfold

Fortunes found
Will often flee
Squandering
With careless glee

Yet caught with care
Gently matured
Can also spell
Futures assured

Reaching for the Sun

What if one could hold the sun
Our burning orb of gas

Hold its heat without defeat
Bear up its godly mass

Untouched by harm and all alarm
Impervious to stand

What would be gained if we weren't chained
By earthly rules command

No warmth known, elements disowned
The sucking void of space

Unknown adrift, unfeeling rift
Unaware of an embrace

Gravity, our locking key
Smallness an inescapable lot

Binds us to this living rock
Purposes a ticking clock

Yet in return together earn
Tenderness to own

Human touch, emotions clutch
Voice of love intoned

What would be lost? Count the cost
To such a power grasp

What would remain of human pain?
Of love? Would either last?

What if one came all undone
While reaching for the height?

Would he burn? Forever yearn
Lost in Heaven's light?

Used Cup

Lift a cup to lips
despite its cracks
crumbling chips

Sip, nothing but air
because of wear
there's nothing there

Disappointing shake
the empty cup can't give
just take

Pour into this cup
attention given
soon used up

Is it all waste?
maybe judgment
has been misplaced

Perhaps all those holes
are there to give
to other souls

Some cups can't be used
For many years
they've been abused

Still, a healing heart
can save the broken
will set apart

Refurbished, repaired
no longer to others
are they compared

For holes can water blooms
provide slow drips
while drought looms

Or be filled with gold
as careful hands
take time to hold

Slow mindful dreams
filling gaps
smoothing seams

No longer meant for games
for wilful use
for selfish claims

Either way its clear
they've moved beyond
your jealous sneer

The Weight of Me

As the weight of me grew
I found myself
Stepping on dreams
Breaking them to shards
Dancing on the glittering
Fragments
Of loss

They couldn't support me anymore

As the weight of me grew
I found I could push
Pull
Carry
Loads that dwarfed others

I didn't always need help

As the weight of me grew
I gained
I lost
I changed
Paying the cost of filling

Often hungry for more

As the weight of me grew
I knew I would burst

Self saturation
Dragging me down
Stagnant strength

I was lost in my own veins

As the weight of me grew
Swollen limbs restricted
Forced to sit still
In filth
Unsated want

Until I'd had enough of self

As the weight of me dripped
I raged
Sweating
Cursing
Hurling up bits

They had turned to poison

As the weight of me balanced
I was shame
Until it rained
Washing clean my ruin
Revealing empty skin

Hunger lingered on

Longing to fill sagging emptiness
Hunting purpose
Seeking strength I once owned

Still
Leery of gorging on self

I still remembered that slow poison

Then you took my hand
And the weight of me
Felt weak
So
You gave me a drink

Homely soup for my soul

I was satisfied
And I shared myself too
With crumbs of words
A sprinkle of laughter
We nourished each other

And the weight of me found peace

Home Over Walls

Let it not be walls alone
But foundations
I lay when pain is near

Foundations anchored
Deep beneath the surface
Swept by hurricanes

The surface cleared
Ready for labour, industry, artistry
Homemaking, husbandry

Artistry layered through
Rafters, hearth, and bricks
Dried within mortar, hardened to protect

Bricks interlocked and bolted
Within the foundations of Him
Who raises homes within hearts before walls

He who welcomes
Nurtures, feeds and names
Those who wander, searching

For names of truth that shine
Beacons from windows thrown wide
To a world that seeks

Wide open arms
And walls that support homes
Steadfast unmovable

Homes that endure
Because foundations where laid
Before walls were raised

Spoken Secret

I found it in my pocket
shoved it further down
down into the folds
where it couldn't make a sound

I pushed it down so firmly
the lining did fray
stitches in the seams
strained, then gave way

The next moment was spent
saving it before a fall
I couldn't bare to see it slip
across the ground to scrawl

I returned it to my pocket
safe and out of sight
it trapped half of my usefulness
away from life and light

Only partial strength
overly cautious will
every task stacking up
failing roles I'm meant to fill

This secret came with cost
dare I let it go?

dare I give it voice
at the world to crow?

I've slipped it from my pocket
still, I'm holding tight
time to make a choice
is letting go what's right?

Whispers from my palm
asking if it's time
calling for a chance
to let their truth chime

Release tightened fist
I catch a glimpse of truth
it's looking like wasted year
withered, fleeting youth

Shaken from my fingers
an object naught but dust
scatters with the motion
shimmers red like rust

Fingers stained crimson
from holding tight too long
still from drifting particles
resounds a simple song

"Hear my spoken secret
I am not okay
hear my spoken secret
freedom starts today"

Lace Curtain

I was looking through the lace
pulled across the windowpane

Intricate
those holes that span
the fabric's skirts

First squinting to look past
at a world wide and vast
than distracted by the dance
of sunbeams on lace

Beyond the tracery, slivered glass
found my eyes a tired host
straining
half retaining ghostly images

Bodies moved
lights flew by
understanding across the lane
obscured, as I battled perceptions

I felt a seconds thrill
but nary the fullness of joy
nor assurance as vision swam
and shadows played

Wasted focus
squandered strength
accepted latticeworks of doubt
until from behind
you drew the curtains wide

And I gasped
at the truth that lay outside

Unhindered

Raw, unhindered
Rising from the soul
It's joy inside a child
It loses all control
In losing becomes whole

Peace Seeds

Not a stillness
Not a stagnation of being
A gentle rippling stream
Moving
Breathing
Living

A wind that breaks her surface
Whispers to the fish
Drops leaves, bugs and seeds
On this
Peace feeds

Taking in
Pouring out
A continuation unobstructed

Battles with purpose
That perpetuate existence
If they cease
Catastrophe strikes

Not an absence of struggle
But acceptance

The rhythm of creation
As it moves seeds forward

Did We Ask

did we ask to exist?
think on it ...
a sentient thought that
could whisper to a woman's womb
"I'm ready"
or ...
perhaps
as the scene was written
the ghosts within the mind of God
asked for life
and he set them free
maybe
we itched within His ear
or twined inside His being
pulling
begging to be
but perhaps not
perhaps we were but silence
pregnant with potential
a question ready to be asked
a lesson waiting for the right scholars insight
and that was He
maybe ...

Hold Hope

I find it
I hold it
it sparkles in the night
the weight
it feels right
HOPE is my might

Look Beyond

Look into the eyes of difference and see beauty
Look into the face of change and see hope
Look beyond normal and find promise
Face the eyes of beyond and find a new bond
A bond, unafraid to go beyond

Wake Up

A tap
———To test the clockwork
————————————Silence
Beneath the pointer
———Test failed

Deliberate
———Compressed lips
———————————Searching for the spark
That lingers deep within
———Determined heart

Expelled breath
———Across the nodules of
———————————Intelligence
Wake up
———Tickled thought
———————————Don't stop

Words of Life

Some are long, some are short
Phrases given, as life I court

I seek to fall in love again
Through every word that I attain

Expressions from my inner self
The paper like a mantle shelf

Words displayed, from the heart
Each a living, vital part

When well shaped they help explain
When disclosed it eases pain

Healing balm on stretching scars
A sharpened file to prison bars

Words my sword to guard my path
They hold at bay evils wrath

Shine a light when held high
From their flame, darkness must fly

A clarity that once was lost
A lifting of the mists of cost

Once again colours I see
I'm finding love a reality

Life has a price, also a weight
Too often it leads us to hate

But if we listen, if we wait
Love will, for life, advocate

Calculated Hesitation

Some view a pause with scorn
Weakness
They whisper
As it stretches their norm

Some view a pause with question
Naming it
Pompous
Masked and aloof

Some view a pause with sadness
Seeing only
Hesitation
A lack of conviction

Some know a pause as more
Restraint
A prayer before
Bravery's next step

Some calculate this pause
Taking time
To understand
Before diving into life's next clause

A list of poems previously published works that appear in this collection.

'Stealing Visits' was first published by Global Poemic, Kindred Voices in the Era of COVID 19.

'Starving Over Time' saw its first publication in 'The Covid Verses' anthology published by Paddler Press.

Thank you to these publications for featuring Mary's work.

Mary Grace van der Kroef is a poet, writer, and artist from Ontario, Canada. She enjoys the simple things in life, like a good cup of coffee and heart-to-heart talks with friends. She uses her writing to highlight those simple things while encouraging others and exploring her own inner world. She is a follower of Jesus Christ and writes from a Christian worldview. She believes every person, regardless of circumstance, is a creative being whose stories are important. She cherishes people's differences and believes diverse stories are imperative to understanding what it is to be human.

Honest reviews are one of the most important things for an indie author's success, and Mary is grateful for each person who takes the time to write a review or rate her books. If you enjoyed this book, please consider taking the time to review or rate it at your favourite retailer or review platform.

www.ingramcontent.com/pod-product-compliance
Lightning Source LLC
Chambersburg PA
CBHW070435010526
44118CB00014B/2044